82

modern
style ideas
to create at home

INSIDE OUT

INSPIRING HOMES WITH HEART

MURDOCH BOOKS

Welcome...

ABOUT THIS BOOK

Inside Out magazine has a long-held philosophy that when it comes to the home, there's real pleasure to be found in the smallest act of arranging, grouping, styling, making or painting. It's a far cry from the necessity of 'doing it yourself' or DIY, and is more in the territory of CIY where 'C' stands for 'create'. In this book, we illustrate the best ideas from the pages of *Inside Out*. Some are simple suggestions you might like to consider – ways of putting things together – as shown by interior stylists with the innate ability to know how to make arrangements work to the best effect. Others require varying amounts of skill, from 'couldn't be easier' through to 'the experienced hand'. Packed full of inspiring ideas, with extra projects from craft guru Tamara Maynes, this book helps you express yourself, update your home and learn from the best in the business.

Karen McCartney

EDITORIAL DIRECTOR

SKILL LEVEL 1: Couldn't be easier | **2:** Requires basic ability with tools
3: For the occasional home project person | **4:** For the experienced hand

TIME 1: Two hours or less | **2:** Half a day | **3:** One day | **4:** A weekend

IMPACT 1: Subtle | **2:** Medium | **3:** High

Contents...

Contents...

home

STYLISH IDEAS TO CREATE...

In every home, we are as much drawn to visual features as we are to areas of comfort.

So, fill your place with these personalised projects that are simple and sophisticated

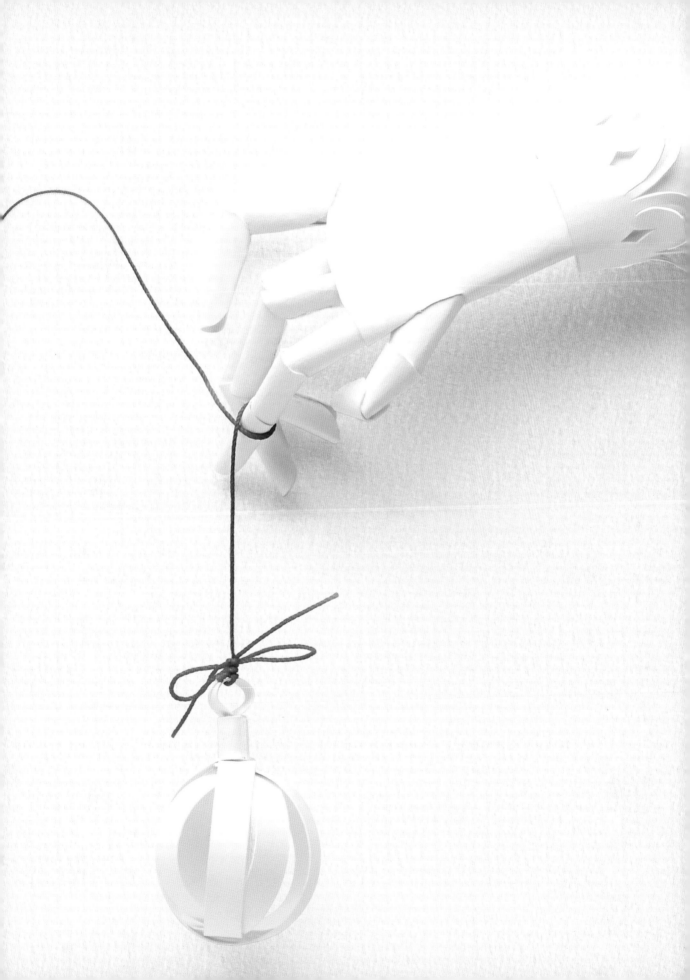

01

WALLPAPER BY DESIGN

Retro wallpaper gets a new life as a floor-to-ceiling artwork

skill level: 2 | **time: 2 (plus drying time)** | **impact: 3**

For flights of fancy, try transforming a plain wall into a whimsical work of art.
What you'll need Wallpaper 'Tree', made of vintage wallpaper by Inke Heiland (glue and brush included), large roll of butcher's paper, cloth, ladder (if you've selected a large work as pictured), and someone to help you.
On your marks After cleaning the wall you've chosen to adorn, place a protective layer of butcher's paper on the floor. Lay the wallpaper 'Tree' flat – tree-side down – and apply glue all over. Then, starting from the base, roll the 'Tree' onto the wall (this is when you'll need your ladder and a helping hand). Once applied, use a cloth to wipe over the wallpaper to remove bubbles, working from the centre out. Attach the wallpaper leaves using the same method (the branches, trunk and leaves of this wallpaper artwork come laser-cut in separate parts).
Tip The project will take up to half a day. Allow the rest of the day for drying. For more infomation on Inke Heiland's range, as well as stockists, visit www.inke.nl.

As an extra decorative touch, position a whimsical birdhouse right in the centre of the tree

Add extra detail to your floor tattoo by painting on outlines with a fine brush

TATTOO YOUR FLOOR

Stencilled art ensures that your most original work is always above board

skill level: 4 | **time: 4 (including drying time)** | **impact: 3**

Decorating floorboards is not only visually exciting, it also camouflages any flaws.
What you'll need Stencil, masking tape, paintbrushes or sponges, acrylic paints, kitchen towel, varnish. If creating your own design, you'll also need a waterproof marker (dark colours are best), acetate, a Stanley knife and a cutting board.
On your marks Draw your actual-size design onto a sheet of clear acetate, then cut out areas to be painted using a Stanley knife. As you cut the stencil, it will become floppier and harder to handle, so start with small details and work up to larger ones.

Before you start painting, clean the floor with soapy water then lightly varnish. When dry, attach the outside of the stencil to the floor with masking tape. Dip your brush or sponge into the paint and wipe most of it off with a kitchen towel – apply too much paint and it could seep under the acetate, blurring the design.

Dab the paint over the stencil with a stippling (dotting) action. If you're doing multiple stencil prints, clean the paint off the acetate after every four to five uses to avoid dry paint clogging the pattern. Just before paint is dry, peel off the stencil. When your design has dried, varnish over the painting to protect it against wear.
Tip The pictured project requires high skill. However, you can choose a repetitive one- or two-coloured design to match your own skill level.

03

FLAG YOUR TABLE

Make a symbolic, evocative or purely graphic statement with a special piece of cloth

skill level: 1 | **time: 1** | **impact: 3**

As a simple alternative to a tablecloth, a flag can introduce a fun and striking element to an interior – and give you a chance to 'fly the colours' at home.

What you'll need A flag with dimensions at least 15cm greater than your tabletop to allow for enough overhang. If this proves tricky, consider stitching a plain border around the flag to increase its area.

On your marks Iron your flag, then simply place it over your table.

Tip Check the washing instructions, as your flag is bound to get dirty.

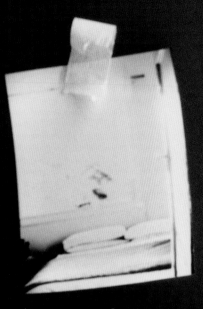

This display works so effectively because the bottles all have a similar, uniform appearance, and the images selected are black and white

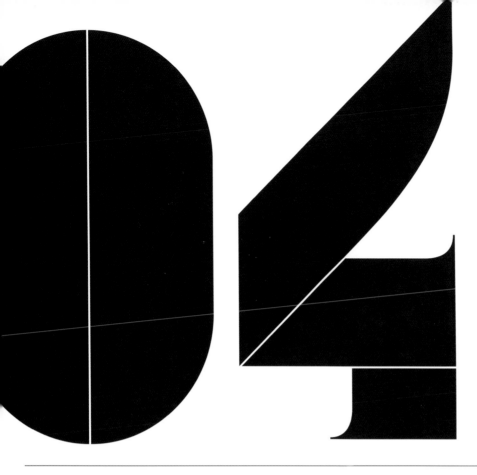

BOTTLE YOUR MEMORIES

This simple photographic display is a clear winner

skill level: 1 | time: 1 | impact: 1

Box frames are an effective and attractive method of displaying your treasured snaps, but sometimes tradition can be a little predictable. If you are after an alternative, this arrangement of old medicine bottles offers plenty of creative possibilities for your photographs. A small selection placed on a shelf will bring a decorative element to a bathroom or kitchen, and even work well in an office.

What you'll need A selection of jars or canisters (preferably in a similar style), a home printer (photographs printed professionally will also work), decorative cards or whatever else you may want to bottle.

On your marks Clean out your canisters so they're free of dust. Print or trim your images to fit in the selected jar. The more flexible the paper, the better – the images obviously need to bend without creasing.

Tip Be creative when selecting images – apart from favourite photographs, try introducing graphic elements such as wallpaper designs or wrapping paper.

05

LINE A CABINET

Create an element of poetic charm that is revealed every time you open the doors

skill level: 3 | time: 4 | impact: 3 (when the cabinet doors are open)

Your decorating style doesn't need to be on show all the time. Lining the interior of an old cabinet, kitchen dresser or bedroom wardrobe will freshen up the unit. ***What you'll need*** Leaves from a book (pages should be thick enough to withstand glue without tearing), sandpaper, acrylic primer, paper glue and Stanley knife. ***On your marks*** Empty out and dust the cupboard, then wash with a mild detergent. Use sandpaper to lightly remove any imperfections. Prime the doors and back wall with an acrylic primer. Leave to dry for 24 hours.

Using a Stanley knife, carefully cut the pages from the spine of your book. A romance or poetry book written in old type will be particularly charming, but any story will do the job as long as it suits the decor of the space the cabinet is in (eg, use a children's illustrated book for a cupboard in a little boy's or girl's room). Covering each book leaf with glue, paste a row of slightly overlapping pages, starting from the top of cabinet's inside back wall and down to the first shelf. Smooth any overhang onto shelf, then continue to cover back wall, stopping at each shelf, to the bottom. Then do the sides, before finally painting shelves (optional). ***Tip*** To be both practical and quirky, cover over any ragged edges or messy finishes with additional pages placed slightly out of kilter for your new-look cupboard.

Handcrafted cushion covers work a treat as birthday gifts for your nearest and dearest

SEW PHOTOS ONTO CUSHIONS

Personalised black-and-white images provide whimsy and personality

skill level: 4 | **time:** 2 | **impact:** 3

Why hide away treasured images in dusty photo albums when they can be used as focal points in living rooms, home offices or bedrooms?

What you'll need Scanner, black-and-white photograph, computer with a graphics editing program such as Photoshop, A4 inkjet printable fabric sheet, inkjet printer, pencil, scissors, pins, needle and thread, cushion with removable cover.

On your marks Scan your photograph and use Photoshop to deep etch the subject away from its background. Resize the image to suit A4 if necessary, and decide on printing placement. Print finished image onto an A4 printable fabric sheet using an inkjet printer. Leave ink to dry completely for 15 minutes before measuring and lightly marking a cutting line in pencil. Cut image out of the fabric sheet, working carefully around the inside of the pencilled line. Pin your print onto a cushion cover and stitch it on, 1cm in from the edge, in large tacking stitches. Zip up the cushion cover and place your work on the nearest sofa!

Tip Adding extra contrast to your photograph will result in a better quality image when using an inkjet printer to print onto fabric.

07

CLUSTER PICTURE FRAMES

Turn the corner of a room into a mini-gallery for maximum impact

skill level: 3 | time: 2 | impact: 3

Add an artistic lift to small nooks or long hallways with a constellation of frames.
What you'll need Pictures, photo frames and any tools required for hanging up frames (hammer, nails, picture hooks, etc).

On your marks Create the bottom row first – start in the corner and keep adding frames as you move away from the centre. Add as many frames – or as few – as you like. Then, move one row up and add your second row in the same fashion. Keep building rows of frames until you're satisfied with the result.

Tip Ensure you have the right drill bits for your wall; double check with your hardware store if you're unsure. A large display will take longer. Also, keep in mind that the size of your picture frames can be different, and that this look works best if you have a mix of portrait and landscape configurations.

You can make additions to the display as the years go by, simply by adding new frames to the bottom row or by building upwards

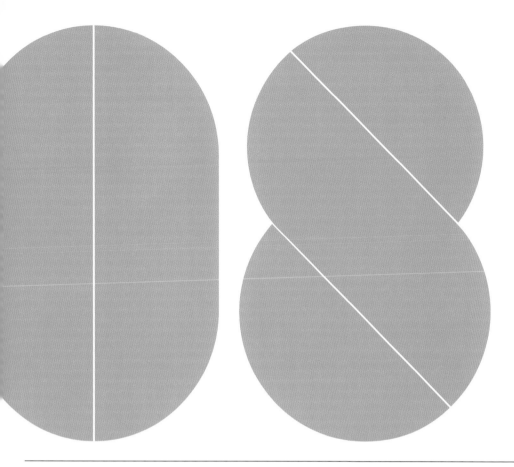

HANG WITH HOOKS

Branch out and display everything from jugs to jewellery with this functional artwork

skill level: 2 | time: 1 | impact: 2

By combining wall art and sturdy hooks, you can display almost anything – crockery in the kitchen, jewellery in the bedroom or bags in the hall.

What you'll need A graphic wall sticker or stencil set, hooks, spray-paint (to colour hooks if the initial finish doesn't suit), a drill and any crucial tools for securing hooks.

On your marks Paint your hooks the same colour as your wall art. Decide on your wall art placement, ensuring you can reach the highest point. Apply your wall sticker or stencil. Mark the wall where you wish to fix hooks (check you have the right drill bits), then attach them.

Tip When positioning, think about what you'll be hanging – for example, you will need plenty of space below if you are hanging necklaces on hooks.

09

BRING THE OUTDOORS IN

This off-the-wall concept flouts the convention of a standard floor-to-ceiling treatment

skill level: 3 | **time: 2 (plus drying time)** | **impact: 3**

" *Take liberties with how you hang your wallpaper or mural. Here, a panel of wall has been left exposed below the mural and by extending it to wrap onto the ceiling, it shifts subtly from wallpaper to artwork. This sense is enhanced by the 3D effect, achieved by attaching small bird-feeding boxes to the trunk of a single tree.* "

Karen McCartney

10
BE INGENIOUS WITH JEANS

Embrace the upcycling craze by transforming old jeans into funky curtains

skill level: 3 | time: 4 | impact: 3

Instead of discarding your favourite blues when wear gets the better of them, extend their life even further and put them to a clever new use.

What you'll need Denim clothing – be it jeans, skirts or shirts – or pieces of denim fabric, scissors, sewing machine and a curtain rod for hanging. Edges along the sides and bottom are best left raw.

On your marks You'll need to cut up your denim items into squares of the same size (approximately 25 x 25cm). For the best visual effect, try to get a mix of squares which contain front and back pockets, seams and plain fabric. On a table or on the floor, lay out your squares into a configuration you're happy with (the size will depend on where you intend to hang it). Pin and sew square by square to form rows. Then sew the rows together, making sure the seams line up, and, finally, hang according to your style of curtain rod.

Tip The most attractive curtain will feature denim of varying shades. For an inexpensive option, source old denim from charity shops.

SPLATTER A VASE

Summon your inner Jackson Pollock and get dripping

skill level: 2 | **time: 1 (plus a few hours' drying time)** | **impact: 3**

Decorating a vase with a few modern paint splatters is a great way to add a personal touch and turn an old or ordinary piece into something special.

What you'll need One or more cheap vases – hunt for sale or second-hand items with bold, confident shapes. (White is the easiest colour option and will make for a strong collection – if your vases are different colours, you can spray-paint them white.) You'll also need acrylic paint, a teaspoon, newspaper sheets and a wet cloth.

On your marks Pour a small amount of acrylic paint into a plastic cup and dilute it with a drip of water – the texture should be slightly smooth but not too runny. (To test, let a spoonful of paint drip: an even, flowing drip is ideal, not a slow, clumping drip or a waterfall drip.) Protect your work surface with newspaper pages or a ground sheet. Lay your ceramic down, making sure it won't roll or move. Scoop up a spoonful of paint with a teaspoon and, in a quick left-to-right diagonal motion, flick the paint across the top of the ceramic. Analyse each completed paint flick before continuing – if it makes a visual impact, leave it to drip and set. Allow to dry and start on the next one.

Tip If dissatisfied with your 'splatter', wipe it off with a wet sponge straightaway.

This look is easy to overdo, so keep it simple and strong for a dramatic effect

Add rattan from craft shops for a less open look and try different types of globes

HANG A LOBSTER POT

Enjoy the dramatic shadowplay that this rattan-and-wire structure will create on your walls

skill level: 4 | time: 2 | impact: 3

What you'll need A wire/rattan lobster pot, four 15cm lengths of fishing trace (18kg breaking strain) with built-in hooks, one-metre-long fishing trace (30kg breaking strain), set of aluminium sleeves (pack of 6), pliers, a few metres of brown, cloth-covered cable, spring toggle cup hook, bakelite-style lamp holder and bulb.

On your marks To rig up the pot to the ceiling, cut off the swivels from the 15cm-long fishing trace wires and clip the other ends onto the four points of the lobster pot's top frame. Thread the heavier gauge trace wire through each of the four lighter trace wire loops and thread the tail through an aluminium sleeve. Form a loop by threading the trace wire back through the same sleeve, leaving a 2cm loop. Crush the sleeve with pliers and trim any excess wire that's protruding. Mark the position on the ceiling. Use a spring toggle cup hook (for plasterboard) for a ceiling fixing point.

Decide how low you want the light to hang and create another loop in the one-metre-long trace wire at the right point, and cut off any excess wire with pliers. Test the loops are strong, then suspend from the ceiling hook. Next, call in a licensed electrician to replace the existing light flex from the ceiling rose with new flex in the desired drop length. Fix the cable to the cup hook by using a small, clear cable tie. Fit the bulb and feed it into the lobster pot. Turn the power on.

13

POST UP YOUR POSTCARDS

If a picture's worth a thousand words, why not speak volumes on your walls?

skill level: 1 | **time: 2 (depending on wall size)** | **impact: 3**

What could be a better way to remember past travels, or to celebrate one of your great passions, than with a wall of images? This display is quite attention-seeking, so it will work best in small spaces – try an alcove or behind a sofa. **What you'll need** A collection of postcards, and Blu-Tack or similar. **On your marks** Once you decide on the wall you wish to cover, it's simply a matter of keeping your eyes peeled for images that will suit your theme. Collecting such a large number of postcards could take a lifetime, so speed up the process by heading to markets and vintage stores where you are likely to find them en masse (and at bargain prices). Simply use your Blu-Tack on the back of each postcard to apply it to your wall, and rearrange as you wish. **Tip** To avoid total visual chaos, stick to one theme, such as statues, travel destinations, flowers or architecture. This not only provides you with a guideline for collecting, it will bring consistency to the total look.

*To increase impact,
use contrasting
materials or
interesting detail,
such as shapely
handles or knobs*

SALVAGE A SIDEBOARD

Modernise a classic piece from the outside in

skill level: 4 | time: 4 | impact: 2

Often, vintage sideboards have great forms and solid structures but are let down by a badly damaged surface. Once your furniture piece has watermarks and scuffs, it's very hard to bring it back to its former beauty. One option is to refresh the outer shell with a sanding followed by a two-pack polyurethane finish, which will not only update it but prolong its life.

What you'll need An attractive sideboard in need of an extreme makeover. It's worth asking your local vintage-furniture store to keep an eye out for you, or hop online and see what's available – but remember, when buying online, it's best to know your product and what it's worth.

On your marks Enlist the services of a specialist furniture finisher (make sure they have experience in two-pack polyurethane work). You could ask for recommendations at a furniture-restoration centre.

Tip When doing your calculations, keep in mind that you may also have transport costs on top of the actual restoration.

15

HANG INDUSTRIAL ART

There is beauty to be found in the disused relics of our cityscapes

skill level: 1 | time: 1 | impact: 2

With the gentrification of cities around the world, the urban landscape is changing. Many sites that were once the lifeblood of our towns – wharves, incinerators and factories – are quickly disappearing, and with them goes a piece of the past. When presented in a spare, restrained manner, such works lend a casual, urban edge to a home's interior.

What you'll need Digital camera, matt paper with white border, bulldog clips.

On your marks For the best effect, research various artists and visit galleries – you never know what you'll find! Otherwise, grab your digital camera, have a wander around a nearby industrial area and snap some evocative images. To produce a large-scale image, take your camera's memory stick to a photo printing lab, and request your image is printed on quality matt paper with a white border. This work is enhanced by the relaxed style in which it's presented. For a finishing touch, the paper is hung using bulldog clips.

Tip The hanging will take under two hours, but printing your own piece can take up to a few days. Double check the lead time with your printing company.

An artwork looks best if displayed with a selection of other contemporary works

16

BE CONFIDENT WITH COLOUR

Spark a child's imagination by introducing a bold colour combination into their room

skill level: 3 | **time: 2** | **impact: 3**

> **"** *Neither dull or understated, this child's desk boasts a lot of elements – from '70s wallpaper to broad painted panels and vintage artwork. While it appears merely playful and kitsch, it's all pulled together by a consistent colour palette. The pops of green in the compact luggage and wallpaper are balanced by the stone hue of the desk light and the wide-eyed ceramic Bambi.* **"**
> **Karen McCartney**

17

PUT YOUR STAMP ON IT

Why relegate these mini works of art to an envelope when they can enliven your walls?

skill level: 2 | **time: 2** | **impact: 2**

Whether you're a diehard collector or a sometime letter-poster, the graphic appeal of stamps is timeless – and the combination of contemporary and vintage is particularly effective on a wall or shelving unit.

What you'll need A collection of stamps with bright colours, graphic shapes or nostalgic value. (Since most stamps are small, they'll have more impact if you buy them in sheets and work with the visual element of repetition.)

On your marks Once you've made your selection of stamps, decide which ones you want to use small and in a repetitive sequence and those you want to enlarge – the success of this display is in the change of scale. Keep in mind that quality will be lost in photocopying to such a large size, but it will also enhance interesting elements such as watermarks and postmarks.

Tip Another creative way to enlarge a small stamp is to photograph it close up in high resolution and have it printed in an enlarged format.

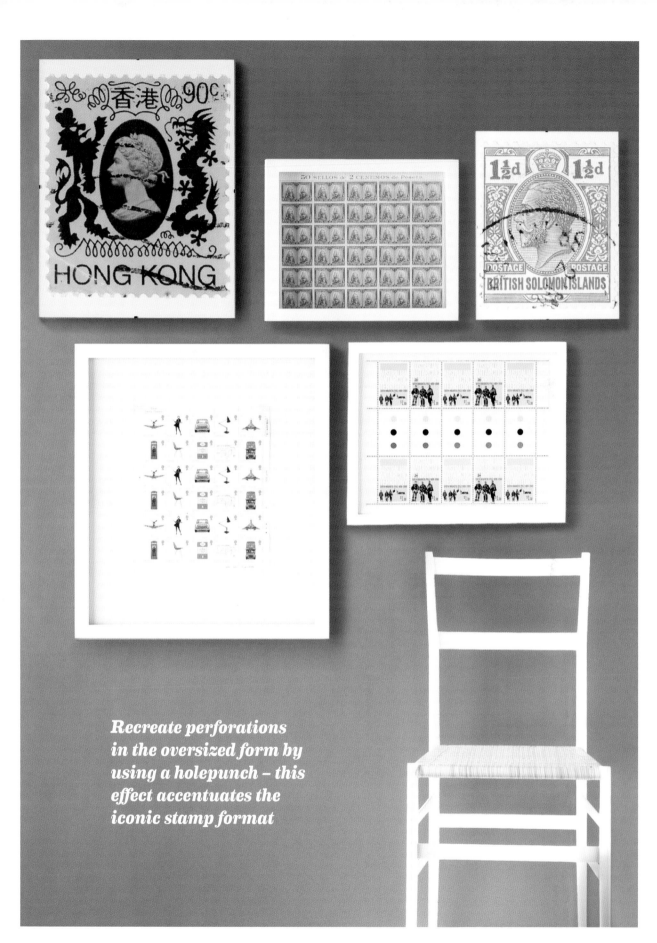

Recreate perforations in the oversized form by using a holepunch – this effect accentuates the iconic stamp format

What do you mean I'm always too busy?
What do you mean I'm always too busy?
What do you mean I'm always too busy?
What do you mean I'm always too busy?
What do you mean I'm always too busy?
What do you mean I'm always too busy?
What do you mean I'm always too busy?
What do you mean I'm always too busy?
What do you mean I'm always too busy?
What do you mean I'm always too busy?
What do you mean I'm always too busy?
What do you mean I'm always too busy?
What do you mean I'm always too busy?
What do you mean I'm always too busy?
What do you mean I'm always too busy?
What do you mean I'm always too busy?
What do you mean I'm always too busy?

LONDON

EUROPA
PARIS

PARIS
NEW YORK
BERLIN
TOKYO

Travel

INK UP

Stamps have come a long way from library dates and smiley faces – you can now press to impress

skill level: 1 | time: 1 | impact: 1

Like kids' craft for grown-ups, these stylish new stamps provide unlimited potential for creating art and personalised wrapping and stationery.

What you'll need Stamps, ink pad, surfaces to stamp such as plain brown paper, painted canvas, shipping tags, envelopes or cardboard (it's best to avoid pattern or dark colours). Try scrapbooking stores for pretty coloured inks.

On your marks Set yourself up on a desk or table with room to move. Have some scrap paper on hand to de-ink your stamps, if required. Secure your surface, pencil mark where you would like your design, if necessary, and simply start stamping.

Tip Do a few test stamps on scrap paper to experiment with the amount of ink you'll need, as well as the pressure required.

19

SMART WIRING

Convert shabby electrical cords into chic, interesting features

skill level: 4 | time: 1 | impact: 2

While we all do our best to discreetly disguise the pesky power cord, there is no escaping its snake-like existence, which most of us attempt to hide under sofas or wind around table legs. Forget about trying to conceal them – it's impossible to do it well. Instead, choose a shade that complements the colours of the room and exposes these cords for what they are. Use colour as a simple way of tying together a theme throughout your home.

What you'll need Two metres of orange electrical cord (or appropriately coloured cord for your home), screwdriver.

On your marks This is an inexpensive job for the experts. You can't do it yourself – unless, of course, you're a licensed electrician or have the relevant qualifications. While rewiring is simple enough in the right hands, it can be dangerous – to say the least – if done incorrectly.

Tip Use a lubricant, such as WD-40, to slip the cable through the tube easily. You can buy these products at good hardware stores.

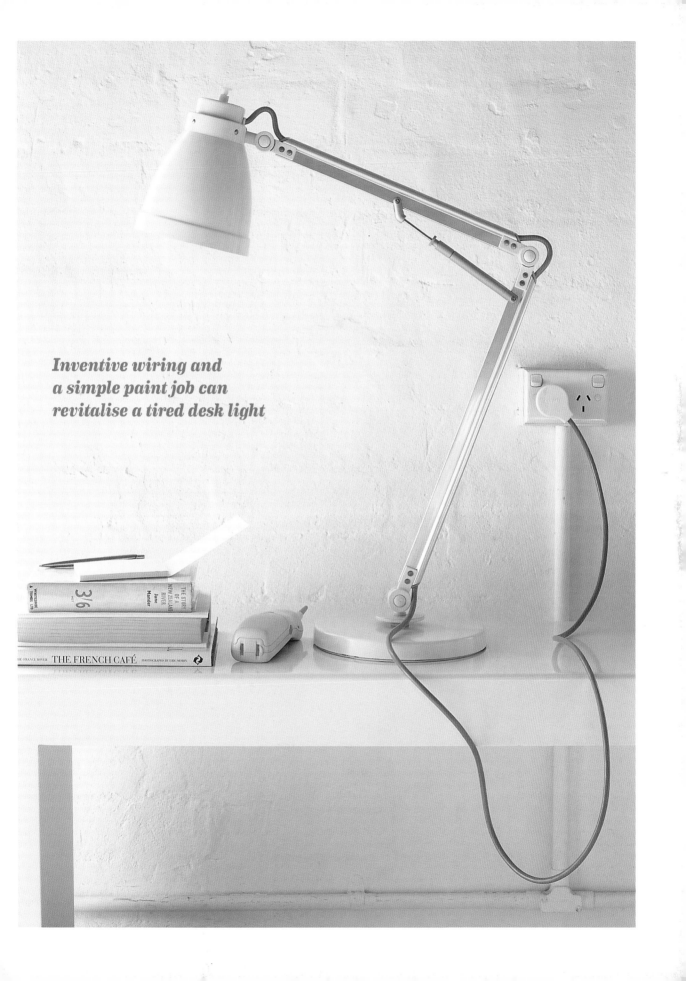

*Inventive wiring and
a simple paint job can
revitalise a tired desk light*

If using boxes as lightweight shelves, consider lining the back with coloured or patterned paper

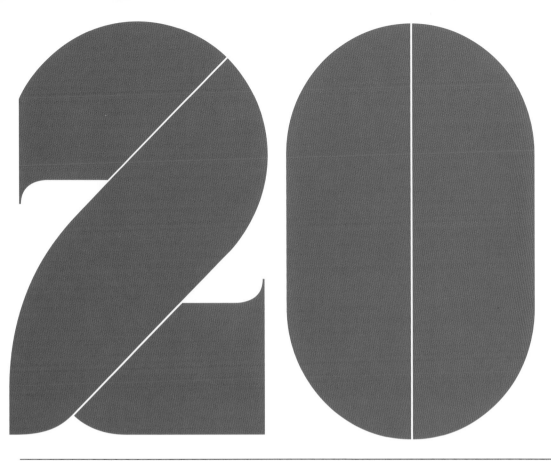

MAKE DECORATIVE BOXES

Express yourself by putting together these crafty cardboard compositions

skill level: 1 | **time: 1** | **impact: 2**

It's time to approach the sticky business of art with confidence.

What you'll need Clean boxes, decorative tapes, scissors, nails or screws, and drill bits suitable for attaching the finished piece to your wall. For quite lightweight pieces, try a strong double-sided tape.

On your marks Decide which side of your box will be your 'display face'. Secure other sides with regular or clear packing tape. Now, start applying your tape design, making sure you can still get inside the box if you need access for fixing it to the wall. Once you're happy with the design, secure the box to the wall. Apply final tape touches when it is in position.

Tip It's worth sketching your design before you start sticking.

this project was made by Tamara

UPHOLSTER A TIMBER STOOL

A timber stool wrapped in fabric is an impressively simple upholstery technique

skill level: 2 | time: 1 | impact: 2

It's one of the most well-used furniture items in the house, so perhaps it's time to give your worn-out stool a mini makeover.

What you'll need One-metre of fabric, pencil, ruler, scissors, iron, staple gun and staples, painted timber stool.

On your marks On the back of the fabric, mark 8cm-wide strips down the length using a pencil and ruler. Cut strips. Iron 1cm hem, facing in towards the back of the fabric down both sides of all the strips. This will prevent them fraying once the stool is in use. Staple start of the strip under the stool's seat and bring up and over the top of the seat. Continue to work your way around, overlapping the fabric strip – like you would make a bandage. Stop wrapping the seat when you get to a leg and repeat the same technique around the top of the leg. Then go back to the seat until you reach the next leg and so on. Use the staple gun along the way to keep fabric strips taut where necessary underneath the seat.

Tip Although they may not resemble their original design, fabrics with larger patterns look most effective when cut up into smaller strips and re-worked.

When selecting fabric, consider other elements in the room – an upholstered seat looks stunning when it has the same tones as other key features, such as a floor rug or kitchen splashback

**Treasured cards,
theatre tickets,
postcards and
personal curios
can add warmth to
a busy home office**

MAKE A NOTICEBOARD

This is an easy way to display your essentials – from paperwork to party invitations

skill level: 2 | **time: 2 (including drying time)** | **impact: 2**

If filing isn't your forte, a homemade memo board could be the perfect solution.
What you'll need Nine cork tiles, paint, large thick rubber bands, thumb tacks, MDF board, small nails.
On your marks Paint cork tiles in a low-sheen acrylic paint. When dry, stretch two rubber bands diagonally across each tile and secure with thumb tacks. Nail the cork tiles onto a piece of 5mm MDF board and hang it wherever you need to declutter.
Tip Colour coordinate bright desk accessories with your rubber bands.

23

SHOW A LITTLE SPINE

Create an instant 'bookcase' with this clever and crafty take on camouflaged storage boxes

skill level: 2 | time: 2 (plus drying time) | impact: 2

While boxes may be handy for storing clutter, they're seldom visually interesting. Attaching old book spines creates faux bookshelves with personality plus.

What you'll need Storage boxes, hardcover books that aren't precious, blade or scalpel, cutting mat, foam-core, extra-strength glue, heavy-duty adhesive suitable for the surface of your storage box. When selecting the books, consider your colour palette – it can make all the difference. Also look for loose spines, as opposed to those that are really tightly fixed, which can be hard to cut.

On your marks Measure your book spines against the storage boxes, making sure they align. Decide on the order of their placement. Set up your cutting mat, then slice the spines from the books – cut in a direction away from the books. Lay the spines upside-down and stick thick foam-core on the back of each one with extra-strength glue. Turn over and, using an adhesive, stick the attached foam-core to the storage box, working from one side to the other. The foam-core adds a perception of depth to the spines, so they keep a natural curve to their shape. When finished, rest the box on its side to apply pressure onto the spines while they dry.

Tip If your spines are too tall, you will need to cut them down to size. Also, you can keep a cover attached to the spine to wrap around the box edge.

For a large feature, try using different colours within the same family and play with different sizes. Then suspend them from the ceiling

CREATE PAPER POMPOMS

It doesn't have to be Christmas to decorate a tree indoors

skill level: 1 | time: 2 | impact: 2

When the leaves fall in winter, choose a knobbly, lichen-licked branch to festoon indoors with these big, bold dahlia-shaped pompoms.

What you'll need Tissue paper (50 x 70cm), scissors, florist's wire, large branch.

On your marks Stack 10 sheets of tissue paper. Fold stack repeatedly along the 70cm edge every 4cm, resembling a concertina. Fold sharply until you're left with a thick folded piece, measuring 4 x 50cm. Cut and fold a 45cm length of florist's wire slipping it over onto the centre of the folded tissue piece. Twist to secure. Trim both ends of your folded tissue piece into sharp points. Next, begin separating each single layer of tissue on both sides of the wire. Work slowly, being careful to separate each layer as close to the centre as possible. This will create the fullness of your pompom. Attach to your branch with the remaining length of florist's wire.

Tip Experiment with slightly different effects by trimming the tips of your pompoms with a rounded edge or using more or less layers of tissue paper.

25

HANG A HALL WITH MIRRORS

Create an illusion of space in a small area by introducing a reflective display

skill level: 3 | **time: 1** | **impact: 3**

" A collection of vintage mirrors placed on a wall can personalise a room. Here, the beauty of this arrangement is found in the variety in shapes and sizes, allowing the mirrors to extend from the door in a light-reflecting grouping. What makes this selection so successful is that the edges are all bevelled, which categorises style and, hence, makes a meaningful collection. "
Karen McCartney

This construction will generally take under two hours, although it could take up to half a day depending on dressing and the time taken to configure the boxes

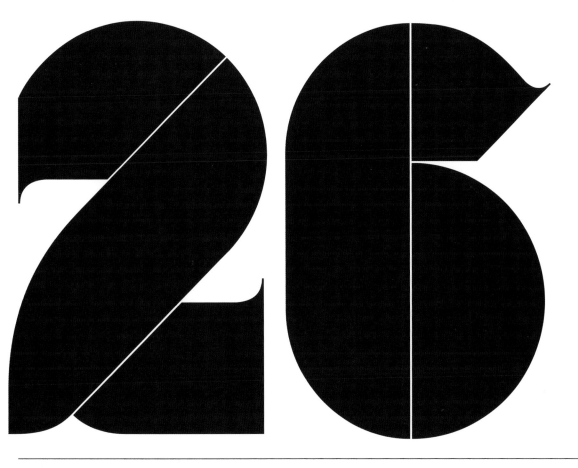

GET CREATIVE WITH CRATES

The humble crate graduates to a sophisticated statement piece with some careful styling

skill level: 1 | **time: 1 (plus dressing time)** | **impact: 3**

This project takes as little as 30 minutes, making it an ideal project if you're new to home styling. The more crates you use, the greater the impact, but a good starting point is at least three wide and three high.

What you'll need As many wooden crates as the space allows, nails, hammer or screws, and drill.

On your marks Experiment with different box combinations until you get the perfect composition for your space. Consider what each crate will house – for example, a tall vase or wide books. Fasten each crate to its neighbour using nails or screws, and work from bottom to top. Use nails instead of heavy-duty adhesive to allow for easy dismantling for future relocation.

Tip To keep track of crate positions while experimenting with different height and shape combinations, label each with chalk – bottom left, bottom middle, etc. It's also helpful to take a photo of each shelving arrangement as a reference for which configuration works best.

27

CREATE AN INDOOR GARDEN

Arrange a row of cascading plants to form a delicate display

skill level: 1 | time: 1 | impact: 2

Here's a modern take on the traditional hanging basket. Placing multiples of the same plant in pots along a shelf can add texture to a room, especially when the foliage spills over the edge of the shelf.

What you'll need Small bulb-like vessels filled with water, small pebbles to add weight, cut lengths of hanging plants (or potted hanging plants), scissors.

On your marks Line a row of vessels filled with water along a shelf. Place some pebbles inside each to prevent them from toppling over. Next, place a cut length of plant in each vessel so it drapes over the edge of the shelf. Trim the ends of each plant with scissors to the length you want.

Tip Most hanging basket plants will work for this project, as will potted hanging plants. We used Chain of Hearts (*Ceropegia woodii*).

For higher impact, use contrasting colours, such as black and white, pink and green, or red and pale blue

BE A STAR WITH STRING

Create a modern wall hanging using an old-fashioned technique

skill level: 3 | time: 2 | impact: 2

Think back to primary school craft projects and string art will no doubt ring some bells. Here, this simple technique has been reinvented using a more subtle palette.

What you'll need MDF panel (90 x 45cm, cut in half and painted), a packet of 25mm nails, 3 packets of cotton tapestry thread (8m each in length), ruler, protractor, pencil.

On your marks To make the large star, draw a 36cm line vertically onto one of the boards, then draw another 36cm line horizontally through the centre, using the protractor to ensure the lines are at a 90-degree angle. Divide each quarter of the cross in half, and then again on either side of the 45-degree mark.

You should be left with 16 points around the circle, which you can number from 1 to 16, starting at the top centre point. At the end of each point, hammer a nail halfway into the board. Knot string around Nail 1 and take down to Nail 9, then across to Nail 3, then Nail 11, then Nail 5. Repeat this pattern moving clockwise around your circle, missing every second nail. (The whole sequence goes: 1, 9, 3, 11, 5, 13, 7, 15, 9, 1, 11, 3, 13, 5, 15, 7, 1.) Repeat the above method to make a new star on the even numbers. (Sequence is: 2, 10, 4, 12, 6, 14, 8, 16, 10, 2, 12, 4, 14, 6, 16, 8, 2.)

Tip For smaller stars, draw an eight-point circle (using 45-degree angles), attach string at Nail 1 and move it clockwise to opposite points, one nail at a time.

PAINT AN OUTDOOR CHAIR

Introduce some Riviera style to your outdoor space with pretty pastel seating

skill level: 2 | **time: 2 (plus a few hours' drying time)** | **impact: 2**

Even the most worn-out outdoor chairs can be easily revitalised.

What you'll need Paint in a chosen selection of colours and french provincial-style slatted timber chairs. While you could easily paint yourself a whole setting, it's probably wise to stick to two chairs to create a point of interest without the risk of it becoming too quaint. You'll also need a medium-sized paintbrush, sandpaper, masking tape, and a large sheet of paper.

On your marks If the chairs are second-hand, you'll need to give them a light sand to strip off any old paint, dirt or rust. To decide on the colour palette, paint some stripes on a piece of paper. Then cut them out so you can mix up the samples to see what colour sequence works best. Before you start painting, stick some masking tape between each slat to avoid getting paint on the frame. Following the order of your sample swatches, paint one colour at a time, allowing all the slats of each colour to dry before starting the next (you'll probably need two coats).

Tip For the best effect, it's worth choosing colours of a similar soft tone. A selection of pastels works well as the tones are different enough to create interest, but not so bright that they become overwhelming.

If you don't have the right nook, put up some shelves to create corners in which to 'spin' your doily webs

STRING UP DIY COBWEBS

A corner of decorative cobwebs makes for a welcome replacement of the real deal

skill level: 1 | time: 1 | impact: 2

Even your dear granny will adore this reinterpretation of the classic crochet doily. **What you'll need** White string, white doily, staple gun and staples, or clear sticky dots or putty depending on surfaces. Cobwebs need to be placed in a corner space. **On your marks** Take the end of the string and thread it very loosely around the doily. Be sure to thread it through the crocheted holes that are as close to the tip of the outermost points as possible. Start installing the doily into the corner from the top, and work your way around clockwise by attaching the string to your surface, using staple gun and staples (or clear sticky dots or putty depending on surfaces). Create light tension as you do so. Where necessary, you can make the string longer or shorter to suit your space as you go around. When you reach the last section, step back and take a look to ensure you are happy with placement before you cut and secure the end of the string. **Tip** Choosing doilies with scalloped edges that are pointed rather than rounded will achieve a more realistic cobweb effect.

31

PERSONAL GIFTWRAPPING

Package your presents in customised paper and it may well impress more than the gift itself

skill level: 2 | **time: 1** | **impact: 2**

While there's no shortage of gorgeous giftwrapping paper available, there is also something to be said for personalising the presents you give. All it takes are some embellishments, stencils and smart scissor work.

What you'll need A selection of papers in different colours and textures, a sharp Stanley knife, gift tags, cards, ribbon or string and any other creative elements you may want to add to personalise your giftwrap.

On your marks After selecting a colour palette (we used pinks and purples, with lime accents), you're only limited by your imagination. We cut out embellishments (such as the name and the satchel) from cards and postcards, and cut shapes from coloured paper, creating a 3D effect by leaving an edge to crease after wrapping.

Tip Choosing a theme helps when purchasing paper or embellishments. Our 'botanical' composition, for example, incorporates flowers, leaves and twigs.

Looking for nifty ideas when embellishing giftwrapping? The myriad stencils and stamps available add endless possibilities

Black with splashes of red will always make a strong statement, especially with typographical elements or numbers

WORD PLAY

Put the writing on the wall, using numbers, letters and words to create bold graphic art

skill level: 2 | time: 2 | impact: 3

In this age of computer typesetting, there's an emerging nostalgic appreciation for letterpress and its unique visual impact and handmade qualities. Letters and words can be used to impressive effect as decoration, especially when displayed as a defined arrangement rather than a collection of random shapes.

What you'll need A selection of letters, numbers or symbols from salvage and vintage stores (or a scanner and printer to copy and print your own typefaces), frames, archive paper, glue.

On your marks To achieve the look, frame numbers, letters and words of different sizes in a collection of frames that are individual yet complementary. Hang, stand or lean your pieces until you're happy with the way they work together – you want the end result to hold some meaning, yet be relaxed and uncontrived.

Tip When putting together a colour palette, stick to a limited range.

FRAME A FLAG

Liberate a nautical flag from the boatshed and put it on your mantelpiece

skill level: 2 | time: 1 | impact: 2

Size matters when it comes to filling an empty wall. That's why the strong graphics and vibrant hues of a framed flag can enhance any room.

What you'll need Flag, large box frame, 6mm-thick MDF, araldite, mounting pins (or tacks or nails), hammer, paint.

On your marks Second-hand flags may be found at auction houses or markets, while many nautical, local and international designs can be bought new from specialists. Once you've purchased a flag, find a frame big enough to hold it. You could have a box frame made, but this may be costly, so consider an old or prefabricated frame that can be customised.

If you're adapting a pre-loved frame, start by removing the glass and discarding the old mount board. Then cut a piece of MDF the same size as the frame. Paint it and the frame in complementary colours. When the paint is dry, refit the glass with araldite around the inside lip of the frame and press down until it sticks. Position the flag on the MDF and attach with mounting pins. To finish the project, simply tack the backboard onto the frame.

Tip If you've snapped up a nautical signalling flag, it's worth finding out its meaning, so have a search on the internet for more information.

INSTALL CUSTOM SHELVING

Install and customise shelving to create a simple yet stylish home for all your treasures

skill level: 3 | **time: 2 (includes drying time)** | **impact: 3**

Is your growing collection of vases, candles and other odds and ends slowly taking over every available surface in your home? If so, it's time to build an attractive new space where you can put them all on show.

What you'll need Shelving, sandpaper, paint, screwdriver, tape measure.

On your marks Lightly sand any of the shelves you plan to paint. This will act as a key for the paint when you apply it. Once the paint has dried, screw the shelves to the wall, making sure you follow the manufacturer's instructions. Then use the tape measure to ensure you leave enough room between shelves for any tall objects or vases (don't forget the height of the flowers).

Tip Paint your shelves in a shade that will match your accessories. The visual impact created will provide splashes of colour and ensure your new display area becomes a much-loved feature of your home.

35

COVER A CUSHION

Give pillows the slip with your favourite patterned teatowels

skill level: 2 | time: 1 | impact: 2

Some linen teatowels are too pretty and contemporary to be hidden away in kitchen drawers, much less used for mopping up messy spills. However, it's their hardiness that makes them ideal as pillowslips. Not only are linen teatowels the perfect size for covering sofa cushions, their simple designs and fresh colours will add that special touch to a chair or bed.

What you'll need A regular-sized linen teatowel (40 x 70cm) with a desirable pattern. If you can only find a smaller version, try making the case with a narrower seam. Alternatively, if your teatowel is too large, start by trimming it down to size. You'll also need pins, iron, ironing board and sewing machine.

On your marks Lay the teatowel flat on the ironing board with the patterned-side up. Fold both of the long ends in toward the centre so they overlap by 5cm, creating a flat surface with a new length of 30cm. Press the two creases with a hot iron. Pin the sides closed and sew them to seal permanently. Reverse the case so the patterned side is visible and shape the corners. Iron and insert a pillow.

Tip You want the teatowel to be snug, not loose, so trimming may be necessary.

Choose linen teatowels with traditional French or English farmhouse patterns, such as ticking or other stripes

Buy lots of different sized boxes from various sources but all in one dominant colour – with just a few in a contrasting shade for dramatic effect

COLOUR CODE YOUR FILES

Add a flash of colour to a shelving unit with an array of boxes in various sizes

skill level: 1 | **time: 1** | **impact: 2**

“ *This neutral, slightly rustic, home office is enlivened by the addition of the punch of colour provided by the stacks of orange boxes. The mix of sizes creates visual interest, as does the attractive grouping – small cardboard boxes work as neat pairs, while larger ones can be placed at both top and bottom.* ”
Karen McCartney

37

MAKE A CURTAIN

Disguising kitchen clutter on open shelving calls for a stylish curtain

skill level: 2 | time: 1 | impact: 2

Not everything in the cupboard is meant for public viewing. For a quick fix, a bespoke curtain can conceal items and add a softness to your kitchen.

What you'll need Fabric piece larger than the console's front, curtain wire that is longer than the shelving, two cup hooks, two screw-eyes, ruler and drill.

On your marks Cut and hem the fabric to fit the size of the console. Fold over the top of the fabric, creating an edge wide enough (approximately 2.5cm) to thread the curtain wire. Sew along the length to close the fold, leaving both ends open. Thread the wire through and screw a cup hook (shaped like a question mark) onto one end of the wire. Drill the two 'screw-eyes' (shaped like closed circles) into either side of the console. Measure the width between the two screw-eyes and cut the wire to fit. Attach the other cup hook over the screw-eyes.

Tip When purchasing cup hooks, check they are the correct size for the curtain wire. They should screw on easily and securely.

Striped fabrics are excellent choices. They add a Bridget Riley-style graphic element to plain or industrial-style kitchens, as the gathering of the fabric creates a rippled effect

If stencilling a whole room, start in the furthest corner to the exit and finish at the exit. That way you won't have to step over wet paint

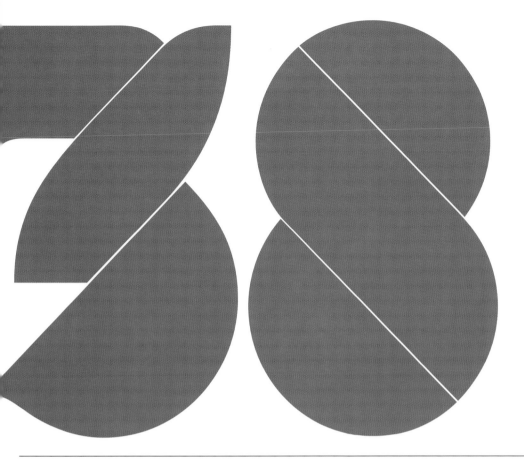

STENCIL THE FLOOR

This beautifully patterned flooring makes a dramatic alternative to a rug

skill level: 2 | **time: 3** | **impact: 3**

Draw attention to your floors with some clever stencilling. It's a straightforward and inexpensive way to add a creative design feature to your room.

What you'll need For the base, try using paving paint. You will also need a small roller, white acrylic paint, adhesive spray and a stencil design.

On your marks Paint the base colour, covering the entire surface of the floor. Once the base colour is completely dry, lightly coat the back of your stencil with spray adhesive to prevent the design from slipping. Place the stencil into position and, using the roller, apply the acrylic paint sparingly. Once painting is complete, peel off the stencil and leave the paint to dry. For a repeat pattern like the one pictured, start from the corner of the room and work across, so that you achieve a straight border.

Tip Take your time over the application process. Remember, if any minor mistakes are made, they won't be noticeable when the design is multiplied.

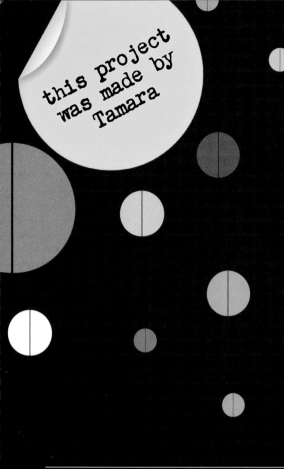

CREATE STRING ART

Why buy expensive art when you can create an affordable option

skill level: 3 | **time: 4** | **impact: 3**

What you'll need 60cm-square 12mm-thick MDF, coloured string, pack of 15mm nails (no head), craft glue, white matt spray-paint, hammer, pencil, eraser, ruler. **On your marks** Draw a 50cm-diameter circle on the MDF, marking points every 1cm. Hammer nails 10mm deep into each point. Spray white; leave to dry. Mark points next to nails at top and bottom centre, left and right one-third down from top, and left and right one-third up from bottom. Tie string onto the bottom centre nail and bring back up to the top centre nail. Working clockwise, pull taut across the next two nails then back across circle to repeat the process. Complete the first layer of the heart by continuing around the circle, ending up back at the bottom centre. The second layer of the heart will alternate between clockwise and anticlockwise steps as follows. Clockwise – centre bottom across to left bottom third point, up to left top third point, across to right top third point and down to right bottom third point. Anticlockwise – bring string around the next nail on the left, back up to the nail on the right of the right top third point, across the circle to the nail on right of the left top third point, back down to nail above the left bottom third point, then down to the nail left of the bottom centre point. Alternate steps until you reach the bottom centre. Tie and cut your string discreetly and secure.

*During the process, regularly stand back and look at the emerging artwork.
It will help you assess which areas need more (or fewer) pages*

ILLUSTRATE YOUR WALL

For an artwork that speaks volumes, decorate a wall with pages from an old book

skill level: 1 | time: 1 | impact: 2

If you have a wall at home that is crying out for decoration, why not turn dusty, yellowing books that have seen better days into an original artwork?

What you'll need A pleasingly aged book (if you don't want to take apart your own much-loved favourites, visit a second-hand bookstore), roll of masking tape, pencil, ruler and tracing paper.

On your marks Decide where you want to position the artwork. It can be long or short – just be sure to leave adequate space around the finished design (about 50cm). With a pencil and ruler, draw a straight, horizontal line (the length of the artwork) on the wall. Ideally, the spine of the book will be faltering and need replacing anyway – so remove the fallen pages and tape them to either end of the line by using small squares of masking tape at the top of each page.

There may be passages, pages or entire chapters you wish to attach. Work in towards the centre, ensuring the pages are the same size and format and layering them to create depth. You can add some contrast to the finished arrangement by including favourite pictures or, as we have done here, sketches on tracing paper.

Tip Choose a book in a foreign language for added visual effect.

41

GET THE WRAP

Impress your friends and family by wrapping gifts in personalised paper

skill level: 1 | time: 1 | impact: 2

" *For a highly individual take on gift wrapping, try photocopying images or text onto A3 sheets of paper. Most commercial copy companies have photocopiers which can blow up images, so even small-sized pictures are useable. Try wallpaper samples, vintage postcards or even pages from out-of-date calendars. You can also use ribbons of any colour to accessorise.* "

Karen McCartney

MAKE YOUR OWN BONBONS

Decorate your feast with these delightful bonbons

skill level: 1 | time: 1 | impact: 2

Bonbons are easy to make and a joy to break.

What you'll need Patterned wrapping paper, coloured felt, ribbon or braid, small coloured buttons, scissors, ruler, pencil, cardboard toilet roll, glue, small toys or sweets to put inside, bonbon 'snaps'.

On your marks Begin by cutting your paper and felt into 16 x 30cm pieces for the two types of bonbons. Prepare the cardboard rolls to be wrapped in paper by placing a snap inside, along with a toy or sweet. As the felt bonbons are purely decorative, you will just use a plain roll for these. Wrap the paper and felt pieces around the rolls leaving 10cm on either end and glue along the overlapping edge. Gather each end and secure with ribbon or braid. To decorate your bonbons, glue on buttons and simplistic flower shapes cut from the paper and felt scraps.

Tip Choose quality paper. The thicker the paper, the better the 'snap' when pulled.

43

CREATE A PAPER LIGHT

A little bit of paper scrunching can create a sculptural work of art

skill level: 3 | time: 2 | impact: 3

If a lampshade is a little dowdy, simply cover it with this easy-to-do paper idea.

What you'll need Stanley knife, white A4 paper, white cotton, double-sided tape, lampshade frame, sewing machine.

On your marks Cut the A4 sheets into quarters. Sew together strips of paper to fit the circumference of the shade. Starting from the bottom of the lampshade, overlap and layer the strips of paper to ensure a dense coverage. Continue to overlap and move the sheet of paper off-centre as you go: this will result in a more textured look. Attach paper strips to the shade with double-sided tape, crumpling and creasing the paper for a textural effect.

Tip Don't paper inside the shade – heat from the bulb could be dangerous.

For a mottled effect, use different shades of paper in pastel colours, such as soft greys or dusty pinks

Neutral or tonal colours will create a sense of comfort and calm, while bright contrasting colours will increase impact

CROCHET A THROW

Hook into the newly respectable craft of crochet for a touch of Nanna chic

skill level: 3 | **time: 4** | **impact: 3**

With a nod to the new craft resurgence, it's time to reach for a crochet hook and create a charming woollen rug. It's a relatively easy skill to master – and it's fun.
What you'll need A pattern book showing how to crochet a hexagon, a selection of yarns in matching plys in your chosen colour scheme, crochet hook, yarn needle and a little patience. Most major craft stores now stock some lovely yarns, but keep an eye out for specialty knitting stores, where you can find amazing options, such as cashmere/silk blends, alpaca wool or even bamboo fibre. Good starting points are wool and cotton, as they are less slippery and therefore easier to handle.
On your marks Set aside some quality couch time and make a big pot of tea. The beauty of crochet is that once you've worked out how to do one square – or in this case, one hexagon – it's just a matter of repeating the process until you have enough for the rug size you require, which is easily done while enjoying a favourite DVD. Once you've completed your squares, give each a light steam iron to set their shape before stitching them together with leftover yarn.
Tip There are plenty of step-by-step books on the subject and helpful online tutorials, so pick your favourite project and get started.

MAKE PAPER BUTTERFLIES

Bring butterflies inside by creating a one-of-a-kind artwork

skill level: 2 | **time: 1** | **impact: 2**

Creative thinking comes to play when choosing paper – different sizes, textures, colours and patterns can be used.

What you'll need Selection of patterned and plain papers, such as pages from old books, coloured paper, newsprint or even sheets of music. You'll also need scissors, double-sided tape and an old picture frame with the back and glass removed.

On your marks Source varied butterfly shapes either from the internet or copyright-free books, then print or photocopy them as templates. Trace the shapes onto your selection of papers and cut out. Fold each pair of butterfly wings upwards to create a gorgeous floating, 3D effect. Using double-sided tape, attach the body of the butterflies to the wall and hang the frame around your artistic arrangement.

Tip Thicker papers will help to create the 3D effect.

Positioning butterflies in random directions, and overlapping some of them, will add visual interest to a bare wall

For a big splash of prettiness, a hot-pink handmade shade will create a cheery mood

DECORATE A LAMPSHADE

When a tasselled trim is added to a drum lampshade, a soft shadowplay appears on the wall

skill level: 2 | time: 2 | impact: 3

Exquisite handmade tassel adds elegance to a humdrum pendant lampshade.

What you'll need An oversized pendant light with a coloured fabric drum shade is required. Large ball of wool (to match the colour of the shade), scissors, ruler, pencil, clear craft glue.

On your marks Cut the wool into 25cm lengths. Work on your shade while it is hanging – preferably at eye level. Measure 1cm up from bottom edge of the shade and mark lightly with pencil. Lightly smear a small section of the 1cm area with glue, and begin to attach lengths of wool closely side by side, covering the pencil mark as you go around. Once you have covered the entire bottom edge, group wool lengths into equal sections, approximately 8cm wide, and tie each section securely, about 5cm down, using another length of wool. Once you have tied each top section, separate wool lengths again into more 8cm-wide equal sections, this time taking half from one tied section and half from the next tied section. Tie each new group securely 5cm down as before. Finally, work around the shade measuring and cutting tassels 20cm down from the bottom edge of the shade to neaten.

Tip Do not skimp on glue. By using a high-quality liquid craft adhesive that is clear and extra tacky, you will make this project speedy and neat.

47

CREATE PAPER BOUQUETS

These creations mean that you'll never have to replace flowers again

skill level: 2 | **time: 1** | **impact: 2**

When selecting paper for this project, anything will work – use your imagination to create your chosen effect. Papers can range from cupcake cases to coloured translucent paper, all in different shades and stocks.

What you'll need Paper media (be creative – any size, colour, texture or thickness is suitable), florist wire to make stems, scissors to shape flowers.

On your marks To create the flowers, cut various circle sizes from your mixed selection of paper media. Starting with a larger circle, place three or four circles of paper together, getting smaller as you layer them. Using a piece of florist wire, about 40cm in length and folded in half, pierce through the centre of the stack of circles. Create a small stamen for your flower by doubling over the end of the folded wire.

Tip Experiment with cutting down into the circle to create a longer petal shape. It's also nice to slightly crumple some of the circles to add a textural effect.

Create an impact with a large display of 20 stems in various heights and styles, clustered in single stem vases or bottles

PAINT A BLACKBOARD UNIT

Chalk creativity up to lateral thinking – and blackboard paint

skill level: 2 | time: 2 | impact: 2

A blackboard cupboard is a cheap and effective canvas for creativity. Apply blackboard paint to storage units and you have an instant chalkboard for scribbles and pictures. Paint a whole cupboard or just sections of it.

What you'll need Storage unit, chalkboard paint (can or aerosol), primer, sandpaper, paintbrush or roller, mineral turpentine.

On your marks Clean the surface of the wood or metal and sand smooth. You may need to prime the surface (if you are unsure, ask at your hardware store and apply primer as per instructions). Stir the paint for at least five minutes before use (and do so periodically during the painting process). With a brush or roller, apply the first coat, using mineral turpentine to mop up any mistakes. Allow to dry for around 16 hours (paint) or two hours (aerosol) before applying a second coat. Leave for at least 24 hours before using.

Tip If you can, position your blackboard cupboard on a hard floor, rather than carpet. It makes the inevitable chalk-dust cleaning easier.

49

COVER BOOKS WITH MAPS

Protect precious books and put the world on display on your bookshelves

skill level: 1 | time: 1 | impact: 2

Decorate your treasured tomes with a book jacket made with world maps.

What you'll need Map, ruler, pencil, scissors.

On your marks First, colour photocopy the selected map several times in order to cover the required amount of books. Place the book on top of the reverse side of the map (blank side) and gently fold the map over each book to cover it. Stand it up and ensure that the section of the map on the spine of each book connects and flows with the spines of the books on either side. This may need a bit of experimentation, taking the map cover off and moving it to the left or right, then placing it back on the book. The larger the number of books you cover, the more a clear picture of the country you're piecing together using the spines will emerge.

Tip Opt for a map that has two strong contrasting colours – such as orange for land, blue for water – to clearly define the country you are forming.

Land masses bordered by seas work well, so choose an island, such as Australia, Fiji or Bali, or even copy antiquated maps, showing exotic lands

Drilling the backs of chairs gives the effect of fancy tooled leatherwork

CUSTOMISE A CHAIR

Fashion a new handmade look for these old, worn-out chairs

skill level: 2 | time: 1 (plus drying time if painting) | impact: 2

Mass-produced timber chairs were once a utilitarian piece of furniture used in schools, cafes or in more modest homes of the day. Nowadays, these 'everyday' chairs are receiving renewed interest, thanks to their affordability and versatility. Not only do these chairs impart a certain 'honesty', but they can be customised in a multitude of ways, from painting to chiselling or drilling.

What you'll need Second-hand chair – scour mid-century furniture stores or have a look on eBay. To personalise it, see the various options below.

On your marks Source a number of pieces with similar proportions and paint them in bright colours for a cutting-edge look, or ask a professional to drill a decorative pattern into the back (as shown here). Weathered chairs look beautiful in farmhouses or warehouses with an industrial aesthetic. For an oriental feel, paint bentwoods in glossy black.

Tip When buying a second-hand chair, check the joints carefully and be aware of models with worn cane seats.

51

DECORATE BY NUMBERS

Take some leaves out of a Chinese calendar and cover a wall

skill level: 3 | time: 2 (plus drying time) | impact: 3

Repetitive patterns or motifs need not come by the roll. This wall has been covered in pages from an inexpensive Chinese calendar, concealing a multitude of flaws and making a feature wall with a difference.

What you'll need Enough pages to paper your wall, spray adhesive with a two-minute setting time, face mask to avoid fumes, Stanley knife and ruler.

On your marks Wipe the wall you wish to cover with a soft cloth to ensure it's clean and dust-free. One by one, spray each page with adhesive and place on the wall, starting from the top and moving left to right so that all the lines are straight. If one goes on crooked, peel off and re-attach. Papering around windows and doors is fiddly so, if you must, cut the pages to size with the Stanley knife.

Tip It's best if all the sheets are smoothly placed on the wall, but a few rough spots or air bubbles will only add character.

*Eclecticism rules
when selecting floral
images and frames.
Different scales, sizes
and colours provide
plenty of visual
interest in a room*

CREATE A FLORAL DISPLAY

A collection of pretty prints and fabrics brings a burst of colour to a space

skill level: 2 | **time: 1** | **impact: 3**

Floral designs have a reputation for being soft and dainty, but if you cluster them in different scales and styles, the result is striking.

What you'll need Collection of floral images, such as printed wallpapers, fabric remnants and vintage prints, collection of frames to fit your florals, iron.

On your marks Spread out your florals and determine which designs will best suit each frame. Larger patterns will need larger frames. Iron out any kinks in your fabric, then cut fabrics and wallpapers to the size of each frame. Decide which way is 'up' and which side is to face outwards, then frame each of your remnants. Style your frames – along with any vintage artwork you've sourced – in a cluster with some overlapping. Position them around a fireplace or sideboard, or hang a few on the wall as well as standing some on the floor.

Tip Some fabric houses sell off old remnants and offcuts. It's an affordable way to get small amounts of quality fabric or wallpaper. A few other accessories featuring floral motifs, such as cushions, rugs and lampshades, can complete the room.

PERSONALISED GIFT CARDS

Identify gifts with this simple stamping idea

skill level: 1 | time: 1 | impact: 1

When they see the way you've personalised them, your friends and family will thank you even before they've unwrapped their gifts.

What you'll need Set of rubber alphabet stamps, inkpad, blank gift card or brown craft card, scissors, scrap paper.

On your marks Choose a blank gift card or piece of brown craft card. Cut and fold to necessary size. When stamping, it is easy to run out of space, so do a test run first to determine approximate letter placement. Once you feel you have a good idea where to stamp the first letter of the recipient's name, do so and continue until you have stamped the entire name. You may also stamp your own name, a brief message or use the letters 'x' and 'o' to represent kisses and hugs.

Tip Don't worry about getting each letter perfectly positioned. Various imperfections will add character and charm.

Dress with a ribbon or string that is finer than your stamping – that way the tie won't overpower it

USE VINYL ON A ROLL

Old kitchen cupboards will look instantly cool with this modern makeover

skill level: 1 | **time: 3 (for two people) or 4 (for one person)** | **impact: 3**

Update rather than renovate by applying self-adhesive vinyl to kitchen cabinetry for unexpected granny chic-style.

What you'll need Rolls of self-adhesive vinyl, cutting mat, metal ruler or quilter's plastic ruler, rotary cutter, set square, pointy-nosed scissors, soft cloth.

On your marks Remove any knobs and handles on the cabinetry and measure the panels to be covered. Using a ruler and rotary cutter (which will give straighter lines than scissors), cut the shapes required. A cutting mat will provide ruling guides to follow, but it's wise to check the corners are 90-degree angles with a set square. Once cut, and before any backing is removed, check the cut pieces of vinyl are the correct sizes. Peel away a few centimetres of backing along a top edge and stick to cabinetry by smoothing with a soft cloth to avoid creating air bubbles. Keep removing sections of backing and pressing down with the cloth until fully affixed. Use scissors to create a small hole to reattach door furniture. Prick any air bubbles with a pin and then push flat with a cloth.

Tip Clean your cabinetry the day before, and ensure it's dry before covering.

this project was made by Tamara

DECORATE CERAMIC FINDS

Ceramic vessels from charity shops become collectors' pieces when customised with paint

skill level: 2 | time: 3 | impact: 3

Group together hand-painted vases and trinkets in similar patterns, hues or shapes.
What you'll need Five small-to-medium ceramic vessels, matt white spray
on primer suitable for ceramics, matt spray-paint in grey and white, small
tubes of acrylic craft paints, fine tipped paintbrush, thin masking tape,
pencil, clear matt sealer suitable for ceramics.
On your marks Prepare all vessels with spray-on primer. Choose a vessel from
your group that has decorative features within the ceramic and spray in matt
grey. Spray the remaining vessels in matt white. To make the lined vessels, mark
lines lightly in pencil and paint over them slowly in one thin continuos line with
artists' acrylic. Use your imagination with the geometric designs and lightly
pencil on your own version. Working through your design colour by colour, place
small lengths of masking tape along the pencil lines isolating the areas you are
painting. When you have done one colour, peel the tape off slowly and carefully
and wait 10 minutes for it to dry completely before you move onto the next colour.
Depending on the artists' acrylic you are using, you may need to do two coats per
colour. Paint all your vessels with a sealer to protect your work.
Tip When completed, it's time to position the vessels on a mantelpiece or shelf.

When attempting a geometric design that requires clean lines, use masking tape as you would when painting walls

CREATE A WALL HANGING

Decorative wall art is a clever way to personalise a bedroom

skill level: 3 | time: 3 (including drying time) | impact: 2

Coloured clay discs can be thread up in an understated but effective artwork.
What you'll need DAS modelling clay, bamboo skewer, roll of cling wrap,
selection of acrylic paints, cotton string or twine, sticks or driftwood.
On your marks Form round shapes and discs from the wet DAS clay and use
a bamboo skewer to make holes through the centre of each one. DAS doesn't
require firing – simply wrap it in cling wrap and allow it to dry overnight. Once the
objects are set, paint them in your desired colours. When the paint dries, decide
on the placement and length you want for each strand, and thread the cotton
string through the discs and beads. Attach the string to the first stick and hang
it from a hook or clasp so you can affix the clay strands while the mobile is
hanging. Carefully add each strand one at a time, making sure you balance the
wall hanging as you go along. Once your artwork is steady, it's ready for your wall.
Tip It's worth sticking to a colour palette of three or four tones.

MAKE A TONAL SCREEN

From apple to olive, this new palette is streaks ahead, especially as a room divider

skill level: 3 | time: 4 | impact: 3

This divider can be changeable in height, width and colour to suit various spaces. **What you'll need** MDF, which comes in various sheet sizes. Find a company that specialises in CNC (computer-controlled) routing. Work out how big you want your screen to be (from each 900 x 1200mm sheet, you'll get 16 large cards or 48 small end cards). A 1.95 x 1.62m screen, for example, requires 111 large and 18 small cards, which are cut from eight 900 x 1200mm MDF sheets. Note that as only two of the smaller end cards are required per row, you need far fewer of these. You also need paint and a roller (paint one or both faces of each panel or card). **On your marks** Draw up the small and large card designs on paper at full size – the large should measure 264 x 172mm and the small, 88 x 172mm – and add a 20mm radius to round off each of the four corners of both designs. When adding slots to the drawing, the large card requires one slot in the centre of the short ends and two slots on the long sides, each 42mm from the end. The small card only needs three slots in total – one slot centred on each short side and one in the centre of only one of the longer sides. Every slot is 4mm wide by 40mm long. The routing will round the ends of the slots. Take the drawings to the routers for computerised cutting. Then paint the finished cards in your chosen colours.

Buy sample pots – the more the merrier, but keep them to a limited palette. Then use a roller to paint one or both faces of each panel

BE BOLD WITH TYPE

When it comes to making a strong statement with a typeface, bigger is better

skill level: 2 | **time: 1 (plus drying time)** | **impact: 3**

> " *Stating the obvious by way of signage can be a striking way of emphasising a feature wall. The words can be in any language and in any typeface – in self-adhesive vinyl, hung vintage letters or even some oversized letters simply propped against the wall. Don't be afraid to play with a character's scale and colour to complete the graphic effect.* "
> **Karen McCartney**

MAKE A TEATOWEL CURTAIN

Stitching teatowels together will achieve a modern take on country style

skill level: 2 | time: 2 | impact: 3

Made of lightweight fabrics, bright and colourful teatowels provide an ideal window dressing for areas you like to keep filled with natural light.

What you'll need Clean teatowels, small window fitted with a curtain rod and curtain clips from which to hang them, needle, threads, sewing machine, iron, tape measure. You may also need some lightweight fabric for backing.

On your marks Iron all of your teatowels. Lay them face-up on a table or the ground and decide on your positioning. Measure your window and ensure that your patched teatowels are slightly bigger than the window. It won't matter if the teatowels are wider than the window as you can trim the sides if required. Tack your teatowels together in strips (either vertical or horizontal), using a needle and thread, with the printed sides face to face. Once all the teatowels are tacked into strips, sew over your tacking with the sewing machine. Then sew the strips together (again making sure printed sides are face to face). Trim if required and sew seams along each side. Hang the finished piece (facing inward) from your curtain rod with curtain clips. If you want to neaten up the look of your curtain from the outside, back it with a lightweight fabric.

Tip To unite all the different teatowels, choose those with similar colours or yarns.

ADAPT YOUR DRAWERS

Who needs a cupboard when you can store items in a drawers-as-sculpture installation?

skill level: 3 | **time: 1** | **impact: 3**

Discarded drawers can turn an unused or awkward corner into a storage area that's interesting as well as practical.

What you'll need Wooden drawers, screws, wall plugs, drill, screwdriver, spirit level, measuring tape, pencil (stud finder for non-masonry walls).

On your marks Work out a placement you're happy with, taking into account the depth and width of each drawer so that none hamper access to another. Drill two holes at either end of the panel of the drawer that will be against a wall. Holding the first drawer in place, check it's straight with a spirit level and, with a pencil, mark the positioning of the holes onto the wall. For masonry walls, drill holes into wall and insert wall plugs. Screw drawers to walls.

Tip Turn one or two of the drawers upside down to create shelves.

61

MAKE A MOBILE

This sculptural art piece can be hanging in less than an hour

skill level: 2 | **time: 1** | **impact: 3**

Suspended from the ceiling, this mobile is made from strips of veneer that move slightly when there's a breeze, creating your very own moving sculpture.

What you'll need Two wire coathangers, lashing twine, 10- to 15-metre strip of timber veneer, scissors.

On your marks Snip the bottom rung off each coathanger and discard the top parts. Cross the two pieces of straight wire and tie in the middle with the twine. Suspend the metal cross at a suitable height from which to work, then carefully punctuate the veneer strips by threading them onto the wire.

Cut each strip to the desired length, then continue the process on the other three ends, repeating as many times as you wish. Take care to evenly distribute the strips on the cross wire extremities, so the mobile remains balanced. Hang mobile from the centre point of the cross.

Tip If you intend to make the mobile a permanent feature, fix each strip in place with wood glue. Try varying the look with different types of timber veneer.

This mobile can perform as a true feature piece. It's best shown off in a spacious area with lots of height, such as a stairwell

This display method also works well for old photographic film negatives

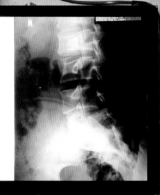
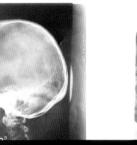

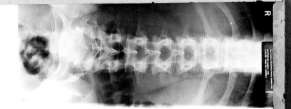

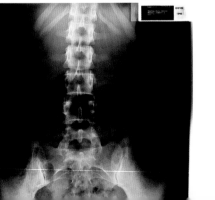

USE X-RAYS AS ART

These artistic X-ray explorations can liven up any space

skill level: 3 | time: 2 | impact: 3

Alternate light sources, such as X-ray viewers, introduce industrial-style light and shade in graphic proportions.

What you'll need Wall-mountable X-ray viewing boxes, X-rays.

On your marks The real work involved here is sourcing the boxes. Look for them in shops that specialise in vintage industrial pieces and at online auctions, such as eBay. New boxes are also available from medical suppliers. The type of light boxes you source will determine how they are mounted to the wall, but there's little more involved than a few screws. Hunt out X-rays in vintage shops – or use your own or a pet's to get some interesting shapes. Place in box, plug in and light up.

Tip A group of three boxes is much more visually appealing than just one.

EXHIBIT YOUR WORK

A slide-in display board can keep business cards, photographs and receipts close at hand

skill level: 3 | time: 3 | impact: 2

Both functional and fabulous, this contemporary message board utilises a 'slot' system – a favourite device for graphic designers. It means precious cards, artwork and photographs remain hole-free, and you don't waste time searching for pins.

What you'll need Sheet of MDF (ours is cut to 700 x 800mm), glossy paint in a suitable colour, seven pieces of ribbed-edge moulding (700 x 15mm), wood glue, hammer and nails, sealer or varnish.

On your marks Paint the MDF in your chosen colour. Glue a strip of moulding along the top and the bottom edges of the board. Measure the business cards, photographs and other messages to mark out the placement of the five remaining moulding strips, subtracting 15mm from the items' heights. Secure mouldings with glue (in lines along the centres) and, for extra grip, tap in a couple of nails from the back when the glue is dry. Coat with a sealer or varnish.

Tip For a more dramatic effect, paint the mouldings in a contrasting colour. At the end of the project, leave the sealer to dry overnight.

For extra stability, adhere each box to the next with strong glue, such as liquid nails

GLORY BOXES

Painted boxes in tonal hues are a stylish storage solution for banishing clutter

skill level: 2 | **time: 1 (plus drying time)** | **impact: 3**

Store away your piles of paper in labelled boxes. This craft idea will motivate you.
What you'll need New or old document boxes, matt acrylic paint, paintbrushes.
On your marks First, organise the boxes so they are stacked in your preferred
order – we chose a step configuration. Then paint a sample of each colour on a
piece of paper and, once dry, position each colour on a box with masking tape
– this helps to visualise how the colours look next to each other. Once you're
happy with the placement, start painting the boxes.
Tip When choosing colours for the boxes, pick up on existing accent colours
already in your room, such as cool blues and greens, autumn colours or pastels.

PAINT A SPLASHBACK

Liven up your kitchen with a splash of colour

skill level: 4 | time: 3 | impact: 3

Take inspiration from colourful tiles and mix it with the easy-clean properties of glass to create a striped kitchen splashback.

What you'll need Paint test pots, paintbrush, low-adhesive masking tape, spirit level, glass splashback to be professionally installed.

On your marks Have the supplier of a glass splashback measure up for you, so you'll know the exact dimensions of the section of wall you'll be painting. If the glass has a green tinge, get a sample as that will impact on your colour choices. You'll be painting stripes straight onto the walls for this project, so before you start, play around on a large piece of cardboard for a pleasing mix of colour and widths. When painting stripes, it's easier to paint the area one solid colour first and then use masking tape to create stripes on top of that, being sure to let each colour dry before applying the next.

If you'd like free-form edges rather than the sharp ones created by masking tape, then run your paintbrush along the edge of the stripe once the tape has been removed. Initially, though, use masking tape and a spirit level to keep the stripes on track. Once paint is dry, install glass splashback straight over the top.

Tip Acrylic splashbacks can't be used directly behind a heat source, so use glass.

When painting stripes, use masking tape or a stencil to get straight lines

CREATE A LIBRARY GALLERY

Picture a fun line-up of children's fiction with the art of book covers front and centre

skill level: 3 | **time: 2 (plus drying time)** | **impact: 3**

When children's books are wedged together in bookcases or scattered all over the floor, their decorative potential is wasted. But placed on narrow shelves with their covers on display, the books are instantly ordered in a gallery of delight.

What you'll need Shelving and brackets (such as Ikea's Ekby Östen shelf, brackets sold separately), nails or screws, hammer or drill.

On your marks Measure out your shelving and ensure that it is accessible and will accommodate tall or bulky books if necessary. Locate the wall studs and mark fixing locations. Screw or nail the support brackets at the marked stud points, then position the shelves. Encourage your child to participate in the book arrangement.

Tip Keep shelves equidistant for uniformity and to create a clean decorative line.

67

WRAP LIKE A PROFESSIONAL

Presents wrapped with ingenuity can provide as much delight as the contents they conceal

skill level: 1 | **time: 1** | **impact: 3**

“ *When it comes to creative wrapping, a considered approach is to theme your wrapping while personalising within the overall idea. Here, strong floral prints have been teamed with vintage buttons, ric-rac braid, pieces of old lace and paper flowers to bring a touch of the haberdashery to gift giving.* ”
Karen McCartney

Keep a look out for vintage lace at charity shops or new lace at fabric stores. You can incorporate vintage handkerchiefs, doilies and cross-stitch

CRAFT A GARLAND

Energise an empty space by introducing a handcrafted decorative garland

skill level: 2 ⋮ time: 4 (including drying time) ⋮ impact: 3

What you'll need White tissue paper (30 sheets, 50 x 70cm), paperclip, cutting mat, steel ruler, craft knife, 6m thick white rope, plastic bucket, fabric dye in six colours, fan heater, hanging space.

On your marks Fold a single piece of tissue paper in half so it measures 35 x 50cm. Fold again twice so you end up with a piece measuring 12.5 x 35cm. Put a paperclip over the folded top edge to hold firmly in place. Using a cutting mat, a steel ruler and a craft knife, make 25cm-long cuts perpendicular to the bottom edge every centimetre. Open paper and carefully separate cut sections on either side. Gather open paper together in the centre leaving cut tassels free on either side. Twist this section, forming a tight rope. Bend twisted rope in half and twist back onto itself to form a thicker rope. Tassels either side will meet to form one full pompom. Fill a bucket with dye and dip in two-thirds of pompom for up to one minute. Hang dyed pompom at a safe distance in front of a fan heater for up to 40 minutes to dry. Shake to fluff. Cut, knot together and hang white rope together to suit your space. Hang pompoms randomly by untwisting to open and retwisting to secure.

Tip Stubborn tassels that are struggling to separate may not be completely dry and will come apart easier when shaken gently in front of a fan heater.

Dress up your dining chairs with this inexpensive decorative idea for a special occasion

MAKE A CHAIR COVER

Revitalise a worn-out furniture piece by wrapping it

skill level: 4 | time: 2 | impact: 3

This tactile cover gives a plain chair a new lease of life.

What you'll need Chair to cover, heavyweight interfacing, thread, scissors, sewing machine.

On your marks Roughly cut pieces of interfacing for each facet of the chair. You will need five in total – one for the seat and back, one for the rear of the chair, and three for the front and two sides of the legs. Secure the edges with pins, and trim any excess material away with scissors. Using your sewing machine, sew together the five pieces at each join. Overlock or zigzag stitch seams. Fit cover to chair with seams exposed.

Tip You can turn the chair cover inside out for a neat hem finish, or simply leave as is with raw edges for a more organic feel.

70

STENCIL A CUSHION

Using an old flour bag as inspiration, create a pillowslip with a difference

skill level: 2 | time: 1 (plus drying time) | impact: 2

While you could source used flour bags, there's something to be said for creating your own in the typeface of your choice. You can replicate words from an authentic bag or stencil something as simple as your child's name.

What you'll need Cotton pillowslip to make your own cushion cover, ruler, pencil, waterproof fabric pen, lettering stencil set available from stationery suppliers.

On your marks Wash and iron your pillowslip. On a hard, flat surface, use the ruler and pencil to draw lines onto the fabric to ensure your letters are all straight. Simply place your stencil set directly onto the fabric and then use your marker pen to colour in the letters. Set your design by washing once in a little salty water.

Tip Ink will best print on 100 per cent cotton (or natural fabrics).

For an 'authentic' aged-look pillowslip, choose natural fabric such as hemp, calico, or linen

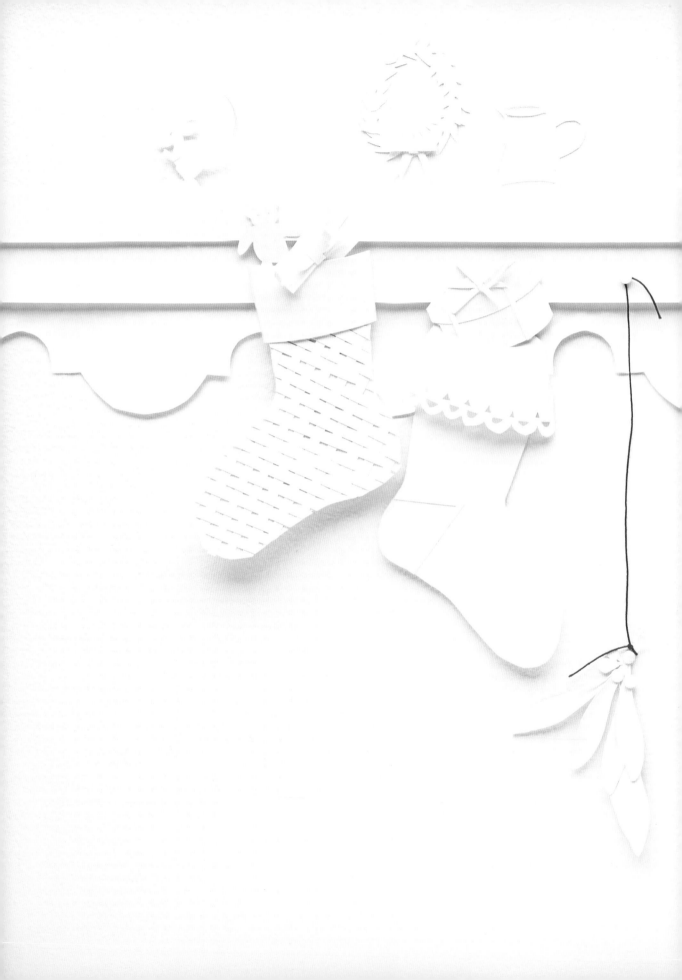

IT'S THE FESTIVE SEASON...

For a new take on tradition, deck the walls with pretty pastel garlands.

Try these delightful handmade candles, a modern wreath, an advent calendar and more

71

A WHITE CHRISTMAS

May your days be merry and bright, and may all your Christmases be white

skill level: 2 | time: 2 | impact: 3

66 *For some, the overload of colour and decoration is too much during the festive season and they'll be drawn to the light, white and spare. To get the look, collect and display a selection of unusual objects, such as oversized buttons, and make a brocade stocking, 3D gift cards, and a pale but interesting garland all in white.* 99

Karen McCartney

Fill drawers with sweets or small toys. For a 3D effect use MDF craft letters instead of paper cut-outs

72

MAKE AN ADVENT CALENDAR

As the contents of each drawer can be changed, this 3D calendar will delight children

skill level: 2 | **time: 2** | **impact: 3**

What you'll need 25 small storage drawers, plain and patterned paper, card, computer, printer, small drinking glass, glue stick, spray glue, scissors, pencil.
On your marks First make templates for the front of your drawers and the circles or discs underneath the dates. Remove a drawer sitting it face down on card. Trace around the drawer and cut out your template. Repeat this step with the drinking glass to make your circle template. Place the drawer template on the plain and patterned papers, tracing 25 fronts. Do the same with your circle template on plain paper. To make numbers, choose a bold font on your computer, print numbers and cut out. Lay out a selection of fronts and decide on placement before gluing on circles and numbers. Use spray glue to secure completed fronts onto drawers.
Tip Using the same block colour for key features, such as the dates, will give your project visual continuity.

73

SCENT-SATIONAL SETTING

A contemporary take on Christmas involves a botanical art installation

skill level: 1 | **time: 1** | **impact: 2**

It doesn't always have to be a large floral display that grabs the attention. There are various ways to give a selection of glass vessels a Christmas feel. This includes adding black-and-white tags that balance the rich colour of the flowers, and vessels being suspended from a branch at a variety of levels.
Karen McCartney

Top your gifts with fresh flowers just before the handover or attach dried flora in advance

WRAP WITH CONFIDENCE

Move on from wrapping in red and green paper by mixing colours, patterns and textures

skill level: 1 | time: 1 | impact: 3

What you'll need Wrapping paper, gift boxes and ribbons in various colours, prints, patterns, sizes and textures, stationery extras and other found or collected objects.
On your marks Start by choosing your wrapping paper or gift box. This is the basis from which your additional wrapping choices will be made. Next, decide on a ribbon or two to complement your paper or box. Experiment with tones but introduce interesting patterns as a point of difference, such as spots and checks, or bold stripes with prints in rich colours. Finally, add a surprising motif, such as a length of sticker dots, or found items, such as fresh flowers. This final step is a great way of personalising your effort while displaying wrapping confidence.
Tip Beautiful cards are wasted inside an envelope. Instead, use their imagery as a finishing touch, just as you would a bow.

DRESS UP YOUR GIFTS

Add final fun flourishes to Christmas gifts with a combination of ideas

skill level: 1 | **time: 1** | **impact: 1**

" *Raid your craft box for textured ties, stamps and stickers, old buttons and new, to decorate gifts and gift tags. Tie up your offering with contrasting ribbon and twine, add a paper garland, or even origami, and finish with a hand-drawn card or gift tag.* "

Karen McCartney

If transporting gifts, remember to pack them well with no chance of them getting squashed. Work with clean hands to avoid grubby fingerprints on the finished piece

CUSTOMISE 3D PLACE CARDS

Normally reserved for table settings, these embellishments double as wonderful gift tags

skill level: 1 | **time: 1** | **impact: 2**

What you'll need Coloured card, tree silhouette (or ready-made 3D place cards), scissors, pencil, ruler, gift box, coloured string, felt tip pen.

On your marks Choose ready-made place cards that suit the gift and/or occasion. If you prefer to make your own place cards, source a silhouette, such as this row of trees, and transfer onto coloured card. Place one upright at the top of the page and another upside down directly below leaving a 13cm gap in between the two. Cut out and fold twice, leaving a 5cm-wide central base. Measure and cut two small folded sections and glue on either end to keep your place card upright. Write the recipient's name in a felt-tip pen and secure the 3D place card to your gift box with string.

Tip Ready-made place cards only come in a standard size, so if your gift box is large, consider making your own oversized place cards.

77

CHRISTMAS STOCKINGS

Even those who find sewing something of a challenge will be able to make these offerings

skill level: 2 | **time: 2** | **impact: 2**

> *Fabric off-cuts, vintage buttons, and leftover braids and ribbons combine to create handcrafted stockings with personality. Simply cut the stocking shape out of two pieces of fabric and use a basic running stitch to join the pieces together. Embellish in sympathetic neutrals or add a hit of colour.*

Karen McCartney

POUR YOUR OWN CANDLES

Fill your home with light by pouring your own candles into household vessels

skill level: 1 | time: 1 | impact: 1

So simple and inexpensive, these handmade candles are perfect for the festive season, but will look just as good all year round.

What you'll need Waterproof metal tea tins and jelly moulds, newspaper, cooktop, candle-making kit, double saucepan, water, ladle, skewer, scissors.

On your marks Place vessels on top of newspaper layed out next to cooktop. Place wax from the candle-making kit in the inner pot of a double saucepan and melt slowly over simmering water. Using a ladle, carefully pour melted wax into each vessel. Wait for the wax to begin to set a little around the edge, then position your wick in the centre using a skewer. If it doesn't stand in the bottom layer of the slightly sticky wax on its own, hold it in place with the skewer a tiny bit longer. Once set, use scissors to trim the wick to 5mm.

Tip Experiment with vessels of any shape or size that can withstand heat, and try adding more than one wick for candles with a larger surface area.

MAKE A MODERN WREATH

Pretty pastels and fresh whites create a modern take on a traditional wreath

skill level: 2 | time: 3 | impact: 3

What you'll need Small, medium and large circle craft punches, buttons, needle and thread, patterned, textured and plain card, sewing machine, double-sided foam squares, heavy card, scissors, pencil, glue stick.

On your marks Draw a 7 x 30cm circular base onto heavy card and cut out. Using the punches, cut out 60 large, 30 medium and 20 small circles from mixed cards. Stick the mostly large, and some medium, circles onto the base. These should randomly overlap each other and the base edges. Next, make the hanging paper baubles. On a sewing machine, stitch five pairs of small circles together down the centre leaving a trailing thread from each. Fan the layers apart before attaching them along the bottom of the wreath. Build the final wreath layer with remaining circles and double-sided foam squares to achieve varying heights. Glue threaded buttons randomly around the wreath.

Tip While these pastel tones surprise and delight, the concept works if you prefer the traditional Christmas colours. Just simplify by playing with different variations of red or green – it's best not to mix the two.

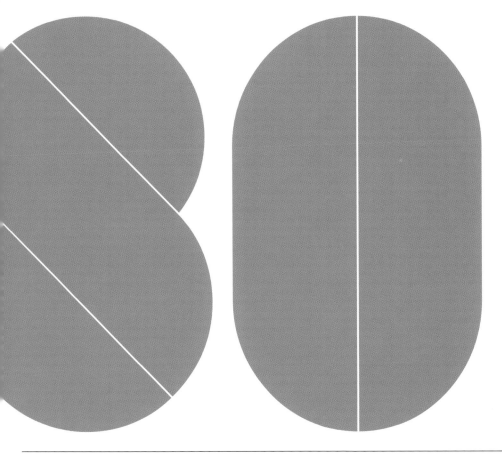

DISPLAY FESTIVE CARDS

Create your own Christmas card curation with much-loved cards and tags on display

skill level: 1 | **time: 1** | **impact: 2**

> **"** *Come the festive season, there are always cards you favour over others – the handmade, the beautifully illustrated, and the cleverly crafted. Here, they have been brought together in a fine wire heart, which allows for a casual display. Concentrate the cards in this area and balance by leaving the shelf reasonably spare with a single card and typographic garland.* **"**
>
> **Karen McCartney**

81

CHRISTMAS COUNTDOWN

Each day in December, delight your loved ones with a message of love

skill level: 2 | time: 2 | impact: 2

What you'll need 25 gift card envelopes, small shipping tags, 25 buttons, large sheets of textured and patterned wrapping or wallpaper, 1m square x 3mm sheet MDF, spray glue, glue stick, scissors, ruler, pencil, needle and thread, number stamp set, ink pad.

On your marks Carefully cover an MDF sheet with textured paper, using spray glue. If the paper isn't large enough, you can join it along the centre. Measure and cut a 10cm patterned paper frame and glue it around the outside of the MDF sheet, creating a border. Divide the section inside the frame by six across and six down, marking meeting points. Date your shipping tags by stamping numbers on each, then stitch through a button while attaching them to the envelope flaps. Glue the back of the envelopes to MDF sheet at points marked.

Tip By using a white textured background, you'll emphasise that the dated envelopes are the stars of the show.

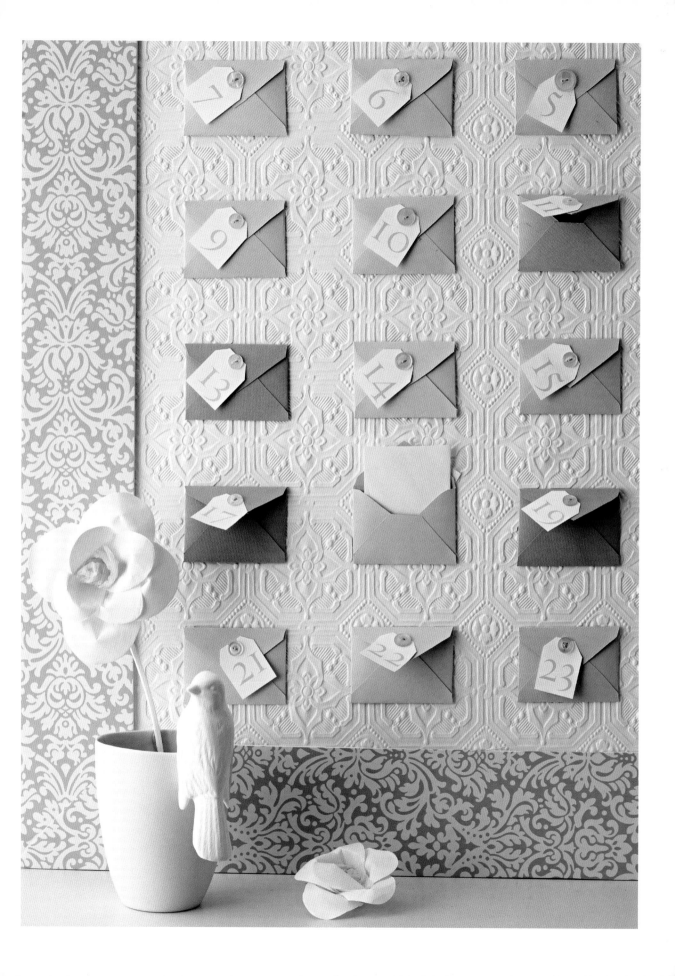

TAKE CUES FROM A GARDEN

Wrap your Christmas presents with natural fabrics and decorate with fragrant flowers

skill level: 1 | **time: 1** | **impact: 1**

66 *When choosing your gift wrapping,
don't forget to consider how you can
stimulate the senses of touch and smell as
well as sight. By taking inspiration from
the natural textures found in the garden,
pretty scraps of new or vintage linens or
fabrics covered in botanical prints can be
tied up with twine and decorated with your
favourite dried or freshly cut flowers.* 99

Karen McCartney

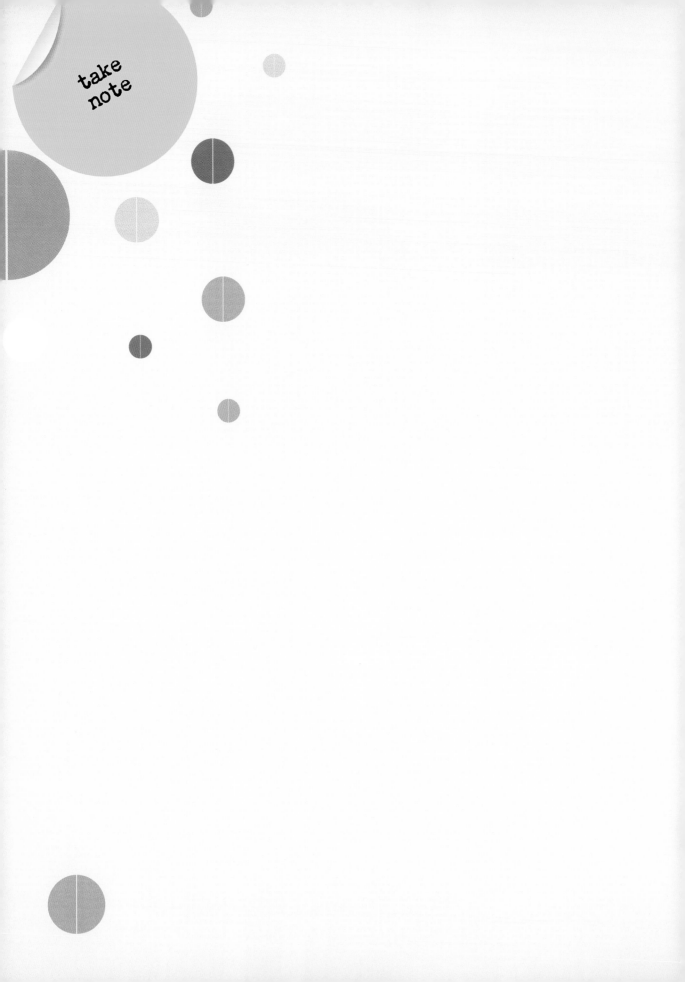

take
note

sources & shops

sketches
& notes

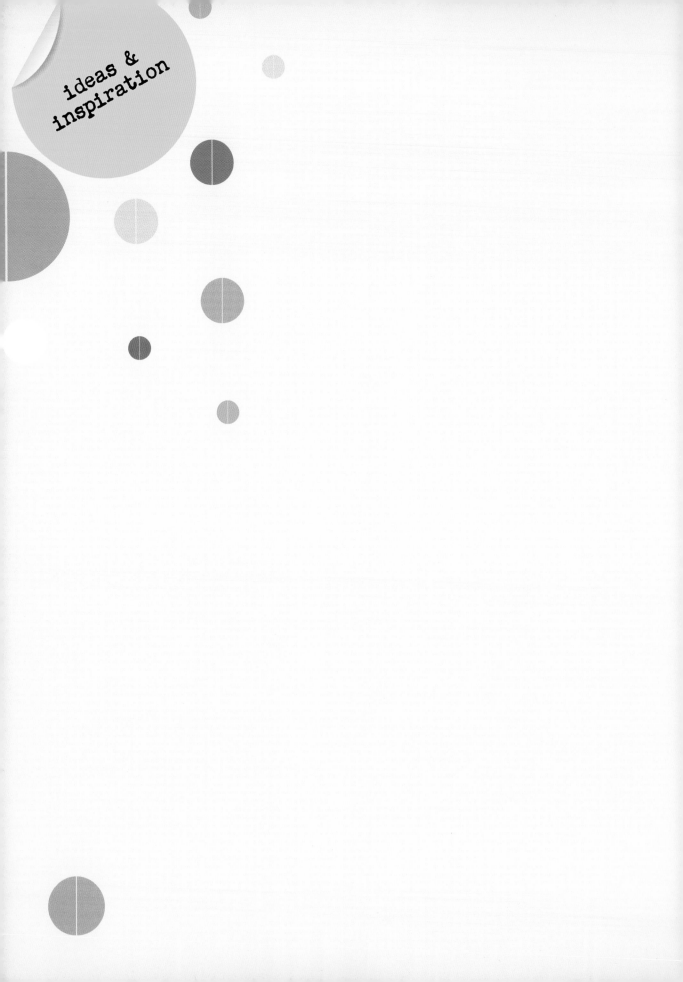

ideas &
inspiration

credits...

Editorial Director *Karen McCartney*
Creative director & designer *Tracy Lines*
Editorial special projects manager *Jennifer Connell*
Chief sub-editor *Kerryn Ramsey*
Sub-editor *Susan Redman*

Inside Out editor *Richard Waller*

With thanks to the following contributors ...

Emily Andrews **65** Mirjam Bleeker **50** Nick Bowers **65** Jason Busch **63** Sharyn Cairns **04, 05** Vanessa Colyer Tay **03, 06, 07, 08, 11, 14, 18, 20, 21, 23, 27, 30, 39, 46, 55, 68, 78, 81** Hannah Delaney **26, 48** Claire Delmar **01, 15, 29, 31, 70, 73, 82** John Dennis **08, 12** Sam Eichblatt **66** Hotze Eisma / Taverne **16, 54, 58** Peter Fehrentz **24, 43, 45, 47, 69** Lynsey Fryers **19, 28, 32, 34, 37, 40** David Giles **25** James Gordon **paper artwork throughout**, David Harrison **12, 17, 57** Saskia Havekes **73, 82** Andrea Healy **51** Lara Hutton **26, 48, 67, 75, 77** Vera Klein **54, 60, 62, 65** Tracy Lines **32**, Lee Matthews **77** Tamara Maynes **06, 21, 24, 30, 39, 42, 46, 53, 55, 68, 72, 74, 76, 78, 79, 81** Caroline Mead **02, 05, 19, 35, 51** Megan Morton **9, 63** Sam McAdam **03, 06, 07, 09, 11, 13, 14, 15, 17, 18, 19, 21, 23, 26, 27, 30, 39, 41, 42, 46, 55, 60, 62, 67, 68, 71, 72, 74, 75, 76, 78, 79, 80, 81** Jo Neville **71, 79** Richard Powers **36** Amanda Prior **01, 19, 22, 28, 29, 31, 32, 33, 34, 37, 38, 40, 49, 56, 57, 59, 64, 70** Glen Proebstel **04, 13, 22, 33, 35, 41, 56, 59, 61, 74, 76** Hande Renshaw **38** Prue Ruscoe **77** Damian Russell **10, 52** Anson Smart **73, 82** Jaya Starke **43, 44, 45, 47, 69** Kirsten Strecker **61** Frank Visser **50** Hilary Walker **44** Craig Wall **48** Michael Wee **51** Polly Wreford/Narratives **35**

82 *Modern Style Ideas* is published by Murdoch Books.
Published in 2011 by Murdoch Books Pty Limited

Murdoch Books Australia
Pier 8/9, 23 Hickson Road
Millers Point NSW 2000
Phone: +61 (0) 2 8220 2000
Fax: +61 (0) 2 8220 2558
www.murdochbooks.com.au
info@murdochbooks.com.au

Murdoch Books UK Limited
Erico House, 6th Floor
93–99 Upper Richmond Road
Putney, London SW15 2TG
Phone: +44 (0) 20 8785 5995
Fax: +44 (0) 20 8785 5985
www.murdochbooks.co.uk
info@murdochbooks.co.uk

For Corporate Orders & Custom Publishing contact Noel Hammond, National Business Development Manager +61 (0) 2 8220 2000

Text copyright © News Magazines 2003-2011
The moral right of the author has been asserted.
Design copyright © News Magazines 2011
Photography copyright © Various contributors (see left)
Cover photography by John Dennis
Colour separations by Sinnott Brothers www.sinnottbros.com.au

National Library of Australia Cataloguing-in-Publication Data
Title: 82 Modern Style Ideas To Create At Home
ISBN: 978-1-74266-678-5 (pbk.)
Notes: Includes index.
Subjects: Interior decoration.
Decoration and ornament.
Dewey Number: 747
A catalogue record for this book is available from the British Library.

Printed and bound in China by Everbest printing Co., Ltd.